Table of Content   **Pages**

AF188624

This note is dedicated to my late daughter Joleen Njilefe Awung, you may have left us physically but you still live in our hearts. May your soul continue to rest in peace, my love for you is eternal.

Preface

In my last publication, *Africa as I see it*, understanding Africa's problem, I discussed some of the factors responsible for Africa's underdevelopment such as poor leadership, corruption and discrimination in the International System like the UNO, WTO and other global organisations.

This note is concentrated on measures that might help to alleviate Africa from inefficient leadership, poverty and encourages economic development.

The problem of Africa is not the lack of good laws as some critics claim but rather the political will to implement existing laws

---

without fear or favour. Wealth should not be a means to escape the wrath of the law because there can be no peace without Justice. Any law that cannot be implemented should be considered as bad law.

Most African governments know the issues facing the continent but lack the political will to address it because of greed and unpatriotic policies. Selfless statesmen like Nelson Mandela and Kofi Annan are needed to push Africa forward.

Acknowledgement

I would like to thank my sisters Mrs Vivian Awung Folefec, Mrs Walburga Efreut Awung and Miss Regina Nju Awung for the tense debate we had that led to the publication of this essay.

I owe a debt of gratitude to Mrs Bunny Seidel, Mr Simon Ndoh, Mr Joe Mofor and Mr Balogun Monodu for their encouragement and support.

The love from my wife, Mrs Cecilia Awung and my two girls, Emily and Darina are great support and inspiration to me. Words cannot express my gratitude and appreciation to you all.

An appraisal

Africa's biggest problems are greed (corruption), dictatorship, and Western dependency. Until African leaders start making decisions that are good for the country instead of self-interest, until Africans are able to vote and fire their politicians, until Africans start focusing their training on entrepreneurship instead of being employees, we will remain stuck in the past. Look at the fastest growing economies in Africa today are those countries that have some limited corruption, some democracy, and increasing entrepreneurship. The more we depend on the West, the more control they have over us. It is not in their interest for Africans to be prosperous because they need us to be dependent on them. They can always point to us and say to their people "you need to be grateful you are not from those countries.......

Regina Nju Awung

Introduction

There is no doubt that Africa is the least developed continent on earth, this is as a result of both internal and external factors. The aim of this write up to is to propose some recommendations that if applied judiciously will help alleviate poverty and encourage economic development and prosperity in Africa, the home of 1,3 billion people.

Africa's problems are complex and complex problems need complex solutions. The major problems facing the African continent today, more than 50 years after the attainment of independence or "self-rule" are bad governance, economic crises, poor security apparatus, poverty and civil unrest.

We live today in a global village where events in one continent of the world might likely affect the other continents. In international politics, states do not have friends but interest. For a state to pursue its interest successfully, she must have influence or authority in negotiation whether in political, economic, social or military issues. The hegemonic and Western powers have an absolute advantage when negotiating with Africa on all subjects. African countries do not cooperate with Western countries on equal ground, the relationship between African and Western nations are more or less like a master-servant relationship. This is because Africa has not built the economic, political and military capacity that will enable her to be competitive in global affairs. This is what Joseph Nye called "hard and soft powers", which literally means military prowess and strength in diplomatic negotiations.

We have witnessed Western interventions in Africa without the approval of the United Nations (UN). The UN is sometimes used like a toy by the United State of America (US), the most powerful state on earth. The US attacked Libya in 1986 and also a coalition of Western powers that include France, Britain and the US overthrew Muammar Ghadafi of Libya in 2011.

Charles Tylor of Liberia, Uhuru Kenyatta of Kenya and Laurent Gbabu of Ivory Coast have been tried in the International Court of Justice (ICJ) in the Hague because of murder or war crimes but Western countries like the US and Germany have committed war crimes in Afghanistan and Iraq respectively but nothing has been done to their leaders. These war crimes by Western Nations are considered as collateral damage or accidents. There is no morality in international politics, Machiavelli wrote that in politics, morality is luxury.

For Africa to stand tall among nations, she must build a vibrant economy, powerful security- military force and establish a closer and more united African Union (UN) that will not solely be financed by the Western powers who crave for Africa's dependency. Africa has the potential to be great and should not limit herself to financial aid and foreign interventions in times of crises. Africa must cease to be crises driven continent. Africans must stop dying as slave abroad due to poverty and conflict at home. African can do better, and there is no better time than now. Despite all the fears of those nations that exploit African resources, I believe that a possible Africa's economic miracle will be good for the world at large.

Good Governance

Governance is the process in which decisions are taken and implemented by states and also in the private sectors of the economy. Good governance is the ability for decisions to be taken and implemented for the best interest of the citizens of a country rather than the personal interest of the head of states or his political allies as practised in many African countries today. Bad leadership has been identified by social researchers as one of the major impediments to Africa's development and this problem needs to be fixed.

Nepotism, tribalism and favouritism should not be the criteria for political and corporate appointments. What is important when considering a candidate for appointment should be competence. Less qualified people should no longer be given the authority to manage state and corporate affairs as rewards for their political support to the government as practised today in Kenya, Gabon and many African nations.

The state institutions in Africa like the legislature, judiciary and security agencies must be empowered with training, funding and independence from the executive so that they can carry out their duties for the best interest of the country and not for the men and women in power as commonly practised in Nigeria and Cameroon.

The influence of Godfather in decision making should be discouraged. Godfathers are political sponsors who exert great influence on their Godchildren for mostly personal interest. They mostly sponsor politicians with the hope to get either influence in decision making or reward in the award of government contracts. Some of these Godfathers try to rule indirectly because of their influence in the society, their Godchildren are sometimes regarded as puppets. Outgoing leaders always look for puppet or Godchildren to succeed them and protect their interest when they leave power. A European example is a Putin-Medwedew relationship in Russia. Godfatherism is a hindrance to good governance because elected officials are not allowed to govern freely. Some politicians in Nigeria define Godfatherism as political mentorship but the role of the so-called mentors have been a source of conflict like the Obasanjo-Jonathan letter "fight" in Nigeria.

The state media financed by the taxpayers should serve the interest of all parties in the country rather than being the mouthpiece of the ruling parties as noticed in the pre-election campaign in most sub-Sahara countries.

SECURITY

One of the most important functions of any state is to provide security to lives and properties. Peace and security are vital elements in the running and functioning of any country. Peter Lock asserted that security is the precondition for economic development, especially today where states are in a serious competition to attract foreign investment. The legitimate use of force should be the sole responsibility of the government. Africa has been plagued with civil wars, social unrest, terrorism and coup attempt from the immediate post-independence period to date. Security is the basic factor for economic and political stability which Africa lacks. There cannot be any meaningful socio-economic and political development without peace and security.

Africa government should invest much in homeland security. The security personnel must be well-trained to face the challenges of today which include terrorism, ethnic conflicts, kidnapping, cyber wars and economic sabotage. The governments must fight corruption in the military and police forces where money geared for the purchase of military hardware is reportedly stolen by top military offices like in Nigeria under the government of President Goodluck Jonathan. Insecurity discourages both local and foreign direct investment. Adequate security provision and social justice may help stabilise some fragile states in Africa like Somalia,

South Sudan and DRC. There can be no peace without social justice. The military and security agencies must be neutral in party politics in order to ensure fairness. In the past, the military has always supported the government in power at the expense of the opposition parties as seen in Cameroon and Nigerian where the military has been used to oppress anti-government parties during pre and post-election events.

EDUCATION

Most African countries should reform their educational system to meet the needs of the local and international labour markets. Nelson Mandela of South Africa said that education is the weapon that can be used to change the world. Quality education is a necessity for all African states. Confucius, the Chinese philosopher wrote that "Education breeds confidence. Confidence breeds hope. Hope breeds peace."

Students should be trained today with the view that they will work after graduation. The government should invest heavily in education which is the basic factor for prosperity. Research institutions should be empowered with funds and manpower to do research that will improve the lives of their citizens. Africa trains civil engineers but most of their roads and bridges are built by the Chinese and Europeans. Africa has some industries but most of the machines are imported from China and the West. Africa has hospitals but most of the wealthy people travel abroad for treatment. I believe this trend is because many Africans do not trust the products of their countries. The quality of education we give to African youths will determine the type of future we want for them. Good governance can only be achieved if the leaders are well trained. No one can compete in today's E-economy without some education. The purpose of education is not to have graduates alone but how prepared are the graduates to solve the country's challenges with the skills they acquired in the university or professional schools.

In Africa, most young people depend on governments for jobs because the private sectors do not yet have the capacity to employ the many unemployed youths. The purpose of the government should not be to create jobs directly but create a conducive atmosphere for jobs creation by the private sectors. This can be done through the provision of loans, training, tax holidays, security and other incentives.

The emphasis of vocational training can help reduce youth unemployment like in Germany where the government has invested many resources in vocational training like cooking, carpentry, mechanics, tailoring and baking. The youth must not only look for jobs after their studies but be given the skills and resources to be self-reliance and self-employed.

Young girls learning model design

The fight against corruption

Corruption is a severe problem in most African states. Africa can only succeed economically if the massive corruption from bottom to top is brought under control. Corruption in Africa has discouraged much foreign direct investments. Corruption is a global problem but some African statesmen like the late Sani Abacha of Nigeria had millions of dollars in Swiss banks while the majority of Nigerians under his leadership suffer from absolute poverty and high illiteracy rate.

Kargo explained that corruption slows down investment and economic growth, the fact that bribery contracts are unlike regular contracts that are enforceable. He added that corruption raises the cost of doing business.

The fight against corruption should be the core of all African governments. Corruption has caused much harm to the economy since money meant for developmental projects are diverted to the accounts of government officials at the detriment of the citizens. Corruption encourages incompetence which is a major factor to underdevelopment. If state and none states workers are paid decent salaries and if they work in a conducive atmosphere, this might reduce the rate of corruption and increases productivity.

Nobel Laureate Rigoberta Menchu Tum asserted that " Without strong watchdog institutions, impunity becomes the very foundation upon which systems of corruption are built"

The African states need to empower the anti-corruption bodies with legislation, training and finance to investigate and prosecute people guilty of corrupt practices no matter their status in society. In order to check corruption among the political elite, politicians and top civil servants should declare their assets before taking offices. Huge penalties should be instituted for people guilty of tax evasion and money laundry. Prof. PL Lumumba of Kenya encourages Africans to put "hygiene" in politics.

Civic education or the spirit of patriotism

The African youths should be taught the importance of respecting public offices and properties because it is for the interest of the general public and not for those who are entrusted to manage them. These youths will become the leaders of tomorrow and need to understand the importance of responsibility at an early age. The corrupt politicians and government officials are simply thieves in power, they are sometimes referred to as pen robbers as opposed to armed robbers. If one loves his or her country, he will not do anything to obstruct its progress as has been done in the last decades. Bosses shouldn't be the last to go to work and first to go home because they are the highest in ranks or hierarchy. The effect of such bad behaviours is low productivity. The carelessness in which public properties are handled in some African countries is a call for concern and culprits should be punished. This laissez-faire behaviour in Africa is encouraged because of the lack of penalties, for instance, constant late coming to work.

The use of technology

The use of technology could be a good weapon to ease hardship and reduce cost in Africa. The use of electronic card readers in Nigeria is said to have reduced the rate of election rigging in Africa's most populous country.

University students can send their research report to their professors through email, this will not only save time and money but the risk of travelling considering the devastated road infrastructures in Africa. Also during thesis defence, external supervisors may also take part live through Skype.

Doctors can use technology to send tests result to their colleagues in different cities or countries for second (expert) opinion through email and even Whatsapp. Patients using pacemaker could be monitored using specially programmed computers. It is now easier to diagnose problems in cars using digital machines than manually.

The use of technology in industries, agriculture and health care will notably increase productivity and reduce cost like in the developed world. However, for Africa to maximise the advantage of modern technology, pre-conditions like stable electricity, maintenance facilities and well-trained personnel must be met.

A strong African Union (AU)

The organisation of African States (OAU) which was later transformed to the African Union (AU) has failed to settle most of the problems faced by Africans like civil wars, terrorism and economic crises. However, the African Union can be a good tool to solve some problems faced by Africans if well structured and empowered with the necessary funds and expertise especially in the negotiations of trade deals and solving of global issues like international terrorism, exploitation of Africa by Western states and multinational companies.

Nkwame Nkrumah realised at an early stage in Africa's post-colonial history that as individual states, African countries will be unable to compete in the global economic and diplomatic transaction. A strong AU will have the soft power to bargain on the prices of raw materials for the interest of members' states. African Union should be the right body to give African solutions to African problems as propagated by some African intellectuals. I strongly support the pan-African view of Kwame Nkrumah and Muammar Gaddafi.

Intra African trade

Africa's integration cannot be viable without a strong economic base and incentives to local entrepreneurs that will make them competitive in the global market. Trade should be encouraged between African states, intra African trade can be facilitated by a free trade agreement and a possible visa-free regime. Some Africans believe in the illusion that all imported goods from abroad are better than homemade goods. The consumption of homemade goods will boost the local economies. The neoliberal policies from the West propagated by the IMF and World Bank which was imposed on Africans have instead increased hardship and economic doldrums. The mass lay off of civil servants, privatisation and devaluation of the CFA in the 90s failed to improve the Cameroonian economy but aggravated the misery in the country. Africa should be cautious with advice and recommendations from the neo-colonialist powers whose sole interest is to maintain their prosperity at the expense of Africans. History has proven that Western economic and political hypocrisy in Africa should not be underestimated in the underdevelopment of the continent. The Western concept of free trade has not helped Africa very much but fair trade will do. However, free trade as practiced today is a mirage, international trade is neither free nor fair.

African countries should embrace democracy and the respect of human rights as the basis of any durable union of people from a heterogeneous origin. The idea of former President Mbeki of South Africa that regional unions in Africa (ECOWAS, CEMAC etc) should be well developed so that they can serve as catalysts to a broader integration close to Nkrumah's vision should be highly supported. One can assert without fear of contradiction that it would be very difficult for individual African countries to compete and succeed in today's interconnected world where negotiations are based on political and economic strength.

Infrastructural development

Africa's infrastructural decay is a recipe for slow economic growth, high rate of accidents and spread of diseases. Infastrural investment should be the core policy of all African governments. The construction of roads, railways, the building of hospitals and provision of electricity will improve the lives of many Africans.

The building of good and well-equipped hospitals will help reduce avoidable death and prevent the spread of diseases. Good roads networks will ease the cost and time of doing business. This endeavour will benefit both the poor and rich. Such capital investment will also stimulate the local economy by the provision of both direct and indirect jobs.

Roads like this one are common in Africa

Developmental assistance

Foreign aid could be an important factor to reduce the poverty and underdevelopment in Africa although it is often attached with strings to it. Assistance from the wealthiest countries can only have an influence in Africa if corruption is put under control. For international aid to meet its objectives, donor countries must accompany the funded project from start to finish through a project supervisor. Experience has shown that most funds received by some African countries from international organisations and partners for poverty alleviation and infrastructural improvements are embezzled by those in charge to execute and supervise the projects.

Most African governments are untrustworthy to the extent that we encourage donor partners of Africa to execute the projects themselves with the home governments as supervisors. For instance, if a country plans to build hospitals in Cameroon, through their diplomatic mission in Cameroon with the collaboration of the Cameroon government, they should award the contract and make the necessary payment through a hired worker as some countries are presently doing.

The donation of toxin materials and industrial waste to Africa should stop. Machines that pollute the atmosphere and banned from Western industries and homes should not be sent to Africa. Africa is not a waste bin for the West because most of its leaders have no vision and interest for their citizens. These donations like automobile, fridges and industrial machines banned in the West are poison rather than help to Africans although they make help to solve some problems.

Real help is the support that aimed at making Africa self-reliance rather than making her dependent from the rich and industrialised nations. Instead of giving Africa food hand out in times of need, Africa should be empowered to cultivate enough food at home to feed its population. Food handout is only a short term help and cannot solve Africa's famine problem. This can be done through training of African farmers, provision of agricultural technologies etc. If this is done, it will not only reduce hunger in Africa but create jobs and boost the local economies. Some critics argue that trade is better than aid, the West should open their markets for African products if they want Africa to develop. Mark Green, a USAID administrate insisted that the purpose of foreign aid is to end the need of its existence but unfortunately I believe that the availability of foreign aid has increased its demand and may lead to dependency.

Global effects of African underdevelopment

The world is today interconnected in such a way that events in one country might affect the other countries either directly or indirectly. Some of the global effects of African problems are mass migration (including refugees) of Africans to Europe, America and the rest of the world. While brain drain is a problem to Africa, brain gain is good for the West. Some African countries like Somalia and Mali are havens to some Islamist terrorist groups that have a global effect. When countries are unable to guarantee peace and security to their citizens, their homeland might be used as a breeding ground for both home-based and international terrorist networks like IS, al Qaeda and Boko Haram. Somalian terrorists have captured international ships in the Horn of Africa and demanded ransom. The USA has used this situation as an excuse to pursue her anticipated self retaliation policy in Libya, Iraq and Afghanistan while Israel has also used it to attack Syria and Hamas in Palestine without the approval of the UN Security Council.

The anticipated self retaliation policy may lead to global anarchy if not well confined, because powerful states may use it as an excuse to attack weaker states for selfish reasons. The UN should be reformed, democratised and given the sole responsibility to act in inter-state conflicts.

The UN must no longer be hijacked by the superpowers. The idea of veto power is undemocratic and must be reformed to meet the aspiration of most member states.

It's said that the Ebola virus was discovered in the Congo but the outbreak in West Africa in 2014 particularly in Liberia, Sierra Leon and Guinea has proven to be a global affair because affected persons were discovered in the USA and Spain. The international support to fight this health crisis is commendable. Most crises today is difficult to localise, Africa must be empowered to solve its problems.

Although the West is interested in Africa as a source of cheap raw materials and dumping ground for unwanted materials, Africa's possible stability and economic development will be a good thing not only for Africa but the world at large. The absence of fair play and morality in international politics is bad, Machiavellism is cruel politics.

Young Africans trying to flee to Europe

About the author

Stephen Ekokobe Awung was educated in Cameroon and Germany. He is a web developer and political analyst. He has written many critical essays and literary works that have been published in many international journals and anthologies. He is a member of the International Society of Poets.

Stephen is a community organiser and executive chairman of the African People's Convention in Kassel, Germany. He is also an elected member of the foreigners' advisory council in the municipality of Kassel, Germany that represents the interest of migrants. Steeve, as he is fondly called has won many awards in poetry and has also presented his literary works in many occasions in Germany. You can please contact the author for comments or errors through email: awung@apc-kassel.com

Herstellung und Verlag:
BoD – Books on Demand, Norderstedt

Bibliografische Information der Deutschen Nationalbibliothek:

Die Deutsche Nationalbibliothek verzeichnet diese Publikation in der Deutschen Nationalbibliografie; detaillierte bibliografische Daten sind im Internet über http:// dnb.dnb.de abrufbar.

ISBN: 978-3-7494-3681-1